MW01096665

Good-Byes

Shelley Rotner and Sheila Kelly, Ed.D.

Photographs by Shelley Rotner

The Millbrook Press Brookfield, Connecticut

To the Faculty and Staff of Smith College Campus School,
1975 through 1996 *and* To the dear people at Broadside Bookshop,
Northampton, Massachusetts. —SMK

To good-byes and new beginnings —SR

Library of Congress Cataloging-in-Publication Data
Rotner, Shelley.
Good-byes / Shelley Rotner and Sheila Kelly ; photographs by Shelley Rotner.
p. cm.
Summary: A photographic essay presenting the many circumstances in which a
child might say good-bye to various friends and relatives.
ISBn 0-7613-1752-X (lib. bdg.)
1. Children—Juvenile literature. 2. Child psychology—Juvenile literature.
3. Farewells—Juvenile literature. [1. Farewells.] I. Kelly, Sheila M. II. Title.
HQ781 .R67 2002   305.23—dc21   2001044919

Published by The Millbrook Press, Inc.
2 Old New Milford Road
Brookfield, Connecticut 06804
www.millbrookpress.com

Designer: Carolyn Eckert

It's not always easy to say good-bye.

 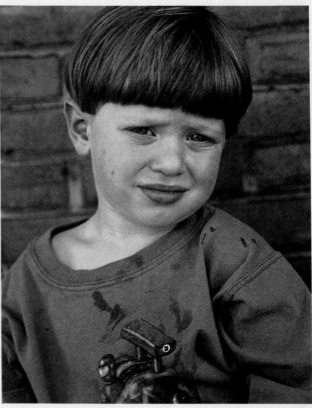

And there are all kinds of good-byes.

There's "good-bye" to your parents
when they take you to school,

and "good-bye" to your friends when it's time to go home.

There's a good-bye to Gram when
you talk on the phone,

and a good-bye
to your dog when
you leave.

"Good-bye" to your driver when she comes to your stop.

"Good-bye" to the man at the store.

There's even
"Good-bye" to the sun.

It's hard to say "good-bye" when your parent goes out,

or your sister goes off to school.

It's hard to say
"good-bye"
when friends
move away,

and you won't be with them so much.

When you live in two homes,

there are lots of good-byes.

"Good-bye" at the airport,

"Good-bye" at the train.

"Good-bye" when you go on the bus.

The hardest
good-bye
is a good-bye
that's forever,

but pictures help us to remember the
happy times of being together . . .

Good-byes can make you sad.

Good-byes can make you angry.

It can be hard to say good-bye,

but most good-byes are
"Good-bye for now!"

About the Authors

Shelley Rotner is an award-winning children's book author and photo-illustrator as well as a freelance photographer specializing in portrait and travel photography. Among her more than twenty children's books are *Changes*; *Action Alphabet*; *Citybook*; *Hold the Anchovies*; *Pick a Pet*; and *Close, Closer, Closest*.

Ms. Rotner lives and works in the New York area.

Sheila Kelly, Ed.D., practiced child clinical psychology in western Massachusetts for almost thirty years, working with preschool and primary school children and their parents and teachers.

She is the coauthor with Shelley Rotner of *Lots of Moms*, *Lots of Dads*, *About Twins*, *The A.D.D. Book for Kids*, *Feeling Thankful*, *What Can You Do?*, *Lots of Grandparents*, and *Something's Different*.

A native of Saskatchewan, Dr. Kelly currently resides in Ontario.